THE
TRUTH WAR

THE
TRUTH WAR

FIGHTING *for* CERTAINTY *in an* AGE *of* DECEPTION
Study Guide

JOHN
MACARTHUR

THOMAS NELSON
Since 1798

NASHVILLE   DALLAS   MEXICO CITY   RIO DE JANEIRO   BEIJING

Published in Nashville, Tennessee. Thomas Nelson is a trademark of Thomas Nelson, Inc.

Published in association with the literary agency of Wolgemuth & Associates, Inc.

Thomas Nelson, Inc. titles may be purchased in bulk for educational, business, fundraising, or sales promotional use. For information, please email SpecialMarkets@ThomasNelson.com.

ISBN-10: 1-4185-1421-7
ISBN-13: 978-1-4185-1421-1

Printed in the United States of America.

07 08 09 10 11 RRD 9 8 7 6 5 4 3 2 1

CONTENTS

"I FOUND IT NECESSARY TO WRITE TO
YOU EXHORTING YOU TO CONTEND
EARNESTLY FOR THE FAITH."
—JUDE 1:3 NKJV

1

TRENDS

"Contemporary Christians are determined to get the world to *like* them—and of course in the process they also want to have as much fun as possible. They are so obsessed with making the church seem 'cool' to unbelievers that they can't be bothered with questions about whether another person's doctrine is sound or not."

—*The Truth War*

Somewhere along the line, evangelicals have bought into the lie that the Great Commission is a marketing mandate. The larger evangelical movement today is obsessed with opinion polls, brand identity, market research, merchandizing schemes, innovative strategies, and numerical growth. Maintaining a positive image has become a priority over guarding the truth. So the message of the gospel is carefully tailored by consumer-relations experts to appeal to worldly minds. The truth is customized to meet the "felt needs" of the audience. Rather than plainly *preaching* God's Word in a way that unleashes the power and truth of it, they try desperately to *package* the message in order to make it more subtle and more appealing to the world.

That's precisely why for many years now, evangelical leaders have systematically embraced and fostered almost every worldly,

shallow, and frivolous idea that comes into the church. A patho-
logical devotion to superficiality has practically become the chief
hallmark of the movement. Evangelicals are obsessed with pop culture, and they copy it frantically. Contemporary church leaders are
so busy trying to stay current with the latest fads that they rarely
give much sober thought to weightier spiritual matters anymore.

1. It's easy for the church to become caught up, competing for
attention in a media-driven world. But the effort distracts us
from the thing we *should* be striving for. What does Paul have to
say in Ephesians 4:17 about those who are trying to keep in step
with the world around them?

2. Christians are often spurned for their strength of conviction, and it's tempting to tone down our stance in order to be liked, to fit in, and to improve our public image. But are we meant to fit in? How does 1 Peter 4:3–4 describe the world's perspective on the Christian lifestyle?

THE MOST COMPELLING QUESTION IN THE MINDS AND ON THE LIPS OF MANY PASTORS TODAY IS NOT "WHAT'S TRUE?" BUT RATHER, "WHAT WORKS?"

3. The postmodern movement offers people the chance to have their cake and eat it too. By picking and choosing what they want to believe, they can claim allegiance with Christ without having to give up any of the things they enjoy. In each of these verses, what is revealed about the pleasures we cling to when we try to personalize our faith?

2 Timothy 3:4

Titus 3:3

Hebrews 11:25

4. In 1 Corinthians 10:7, how does Paul refer to those whose only concern is the pleasure to be found in food and fun?

5. What is the destiny of those who continuously fill their minds with earthly things, according to Philippians 3:19?

6. What real danger do the pleasures of life hold for our spiritual life according to Luke 8:14?

7. Believers are not called to fit in, but to stand out from the rest of the world. How does Jesus describe those who belong to Him in Matthew 5:14?

8. How does Peter refer to those who have chosen to follow God in 1 Peter 2:9?

> "MANY MEGACHURCHES PURPOSEFULLY CATER TO THE PREFERENCES OF THE UNGODLY— FURNISHING ENTERTAINMENT AND AMUSEMENTS IN PLACE OF AUTHENTIC WORSHIP AND BIBLE TEACHING."

It has been suggested that postmodernism is something the church should embrace and adopt. Proponents insist that Christians at least need to start speaking the postmodern dialect if we want to reach a postmodern generation. In order to speak this new language, it will require a complete retooling of the message we bring to the world. They say that Christian theology therefore needs to be rethought, revised, and adapted in order to keep in step and remain relevant in these changing times.

9. So despite modern trends, we need not attempt to keep in step with the world. What is the biblical alternative suggested by 1 Peter 2:21?

10. There are promises in Scripture for those whose steps follow the Lord's in faithfulness. How do each of these verses strengthen your resolve to walk in truth?

Psalm 37:23

Psalm 37:31

Psalm 85:13

11. Though the trend of postmodernism is luring people away from the path God has directed us into, Scripture calls us to take care how we walk. What are our two options, according to Romans 8:1?

12. Paul uses the idea of walking repeatedly in his epistles when he speaks of the lives we live. His longing was for those who followed after Jesus to carry out their days in a manner worthy of the Lord they professed to follow. See if you can discern which of the following statements is true or false, basing your answer on the accompanying Scripture.

___ Because God has called us, we should make an effort to live worthy of His calling (1 Thess. 2:12).

___ We should live our lives without a care as to what anybody else thinks of us (1 Thess. 4:12).

___ The way we act points to what we really think about stuff (Gal. 5:25).

___ As individuals, we must be true to ourselves. Nothing should guide us but our own hearts (Eph. 4:1).

___ Now that we've been saved, everything has changed. There's no going back (Eph. 5:8).

13. In Colossians 1:10, Paul expounds a little on what a worthy walk looks like. How do you see yourself living up to his prayer for your life?

"IN THE EMERGING CHURCH MOVEMENT, TRUTH IS ASSUMED TO BE INHERENTLY HAZY, INDISTINCT, AND UNCERTAIN—PERHAPS EVEN ULTIMATELY UNKNOWABLE."

With increasing frequency nowadays, I hear people say things like, "Come, now, let's not bicker about what we believe. It's only doctrine. Let's focus instead on how we live. The *way* of Jesus is surely more important than our arguments over the *words* of Jesus. Let's set aside our disagreements over creeds and dogmas and devote ourselves instead to showing the love of Christ by the way we conduct our lives." On the face of it, it sounds generous, kind-hearted, modest, and altruistic, but what does the Word of God say about an attitude like this?

"THE BEDROCK CONVICTIONS OF BIBLICAL CHRISTIANITY—SUCH AS FIRM BELIEF IN THE INSPIRATION AND AUTHORITY OF SCRIPTURE, A SOUND UNDERSTANDING OF THE TRUE GOSPEL, FULL ASSURANCE OF SALVATION, SETTLED CONFIDENCE IN THE LORDSHIP OF CHRIST, AND THE NARROW EXCLUSIVITY OF CHRIST AS THE ONLY WAY OF SALVATION—DO NOT RECONCILE WELL WITH POSTMODERNISM'S CONTEMPT FOR CLEAR, AUTHORITATIVE TRUTH-CLAIMS."

14. We live in a world where being sure of anything is considered completely arrogant. It's better to be tolerant, open-minded, and accepting of all views. To say any one thing is the only truth is downright rude. How does Paul describe this kind of mindset in Ephesians 4:14?

15. Right and wrong have been redefined in terms of subjective feelings and personal perspectives. But all the rationalization in the world cannot change foolishness into truth. What does Isaiah 32:6 say that the foolish person will do?

16. In an effort to establish themselves as "good, moral people," many have sought to create their own truth to live by. This is nothing new. How does Paul describe these folks in Romans 10:3?

17. Just because a philosophy (like postmodernism) is empty and baseless doesn't mean that it can't do serious damage. What warning does Paul bring before us in Colossians 2:8 about such things?

18. Those who are accustomed to having their own way in life are reluctant to let go of that control. Instead of acknowledging the truth, they hunt around for those who will validate what they already believe. What does 2 Timothy 4:3–4 say has happened?

2

DECEPTIONS

"Apostate false teachers are not humble. They are not broken. They are not submissive. They are not meek. They are blatant, proud, sovereigns of their own religious empires. And while they like to use Christ's name for their advantage, they do not really know, obey, or love the truth—written or Incarnate."

—The Truth War

Contemporary evangelicalism seems bent on shaping itself into the most stylish, trendy movement in the history of the church. Old certainties are often met with automatic suspicion just because they have been assumed by generation after generation of evangelicals. These days it's fashionable to question *everything*.

This is true of all apostates. At the heart of their apostasy is rebellion against Christ's lordship. Even if they confess with their lips, they deny with their lives. They may call Jesus, "Lord, Lord" but they do not do what He says (Luke 6:46). Their apostasy eventually poisons all their doctrine. They twist and pervert and reinvent teachings of Christ. They adjust the gospel to suit their own tastes. When you get to the core of where they are, they simply want to be kings of their own domains.

1. Virtually all the major epistles in the New Testament address the problem of false teachers in one way or another. What warnings does Paul send to his young protégé in his letters?

1 Timothy 1:4

1 Timothy 6:20

2. It should come as no surprise that false teachers are in the midst of the church even now. From the very beginning, people tried to twist and tamper with the truth of the gospel. See if you can discern which of the following statements is true or false, basing your answer on the accompanying Scripture.

____ False teachers can be spotted a mile away because of their sinister appearances (2 Cor. 11:13–15).

____ Unfortunately, false teachers will be quite effective, and many will be drawn to them (2 Pet. 2:2).

____ There is absolutely no cause for concern that deceivers are at work right now within the church (Acts 20:30).

___ Traditions should hold as much weight as doctrinal teachings when it comes to spiritual life (Matt. 15:1–3).

___ Satan has any number of devices at his disposal to deceive the ignorant (2 Cor. 2:11).

___ Tolerance is key. We shouldn't worry about those who are spreading false doctrines (Titus 1:11).

___ Even within the church there will be those who will try to deceive and exploit others (2 Pet. 2:3).

___ Sometimes a veneer of righteousness is all that stands between what we think we see and what is really true (2 Cor. 11:13).

___ Once someone learns the truth of salvation, they would never want to turn down the gift of grace (2 Tim. 3:8).

___ We should test the words of our teachers to see if they are in accordance with the truth (Isa. 8:20).

3. Too many have decided it's easier and seems so much "nicer" to pretend *every* doctrinal deviation is ultimately insignificant. What does Hebrews 13:9 urge us to do in the face of strange doctrines?

4. The church is not supposed to ape the world's fads or court the world's favor. Why would such behavior be pointless anyhow, according to John 15:18–19?

5. Read Paul's words in Romans 16:17–18. With his warning in mind, answer this quick series of questions:

"THE MESSAGE COMING FROM POSTMODERNIZED EVANGELICALS OPPOSES THE TRUTH: CERTAINTY IS OVERRATED. ASSURANCE IS ARROGANT. BETTER TO KEEP CHANGING YOUR MIND AND KEEP YOUR THEOLOGY IN A CONSTANT STATE OF FLUX."

Who do the teachers of contrary doctrines serve?

How are they able to convince people into believing them?

Who is most vulnerable to their smooth talking?

What is Paul's preferred method of dealing with these false teachers?

6. When it comes right down to it, false teachers are hypocrites. They use pretty words to say all the right things, but their hearts are filled with selfish plans and ulterior motives. How does Ezekiel 33:31–32 show the contrast between outward appearances and the plain truth?

"BY FAR THE GREATEST DANGER FACING THE CHURCH TODAY IS UTTER APATHY TOWARD THE TRUTH AND INDIFFERENCE ABOUT FALSE TEACHING."

7. Jesus reiterated this truth about hypocrites when confronted with the skewed doctrines of the Pharisees in Matthew 15:7–9. What contradictions in their lives did He bring to light?

8. According to James 1:22, what do we need to be?

9. What kind of people does Paul warn us away from in
2 Timothy 3:5?

10. Such people work hard to deceive others, and in the process,
they deceive themselves as well.

What does Proverbs 12:15 say is this kind of person's basis for
living?

How does Psalm 10:11 say such people rationalize their activities?

What do the people in Romans 1:32 persist in doing, though they know better?

"PIOUS ACTIONS DEVOID OF ANY REAL LOVE FOR THE TRUTH DO NOT EVEN CONSTITUTE GENUINE 'ORTHOPRAXY' BY ANY MEASURE. ON THE CONTRARY; THAT'S THE WORST KIND OF SELF-RIGHTEOUS HYPOCRISY."

One of postmodernism's deceptions is the elevation of ortho-praxy over orthodoxy. In other words, insisting that doing good is more valuable than knowing what is right. It is not kindness at all, but the worst form of cruelty, to suggest that what people believe doesn't really matter much if they feel spiritual and do good. In fact, on the face of it, that claim is a blatant contradiction of the gospel message. Scripture clearly and consistently teaches the primacy of right belief as the foundation of right behavior. In other words, righteous living is properly seen as a fruit of authentic faith, and never the other way around. Biblical orthodoxy encompasses orthopraxy. *Both* right doctrine and right living are absolutely essential and totally inseparable for the true child of God.

"SOME OF THE GREATEST THREATS TO TRUTH TODAY COME FROM WITHIN THE VISIBLE CHURCH. APOSTATES AND FALSE TEACHERS ARE THERE IN VAST ABUNDANCE— TEACHING LIES, POPULARIZING GROSS FALSEHOODS, REINVENTING ESSENTIAL DOCTRINES, AND EVEN REDEFINING TRUTH ITSELF."

11. Real righteousness simply cannot exist in isolation from belief in the truth. If you try to separate what makes a "good, moral life" from biblical doctrine, you have to remove any hint of true righteousness from the definition of *good*. Consider the following statements and see if you can discern which is true or false, basing your answer on the accompanying Scripture.

____ The good things we do are evidence of the vibrancy and vitality of our faith (James 2:26).

____ In order to be a true follower of Jesus, you need to know exactly what He taught. Vague ideals aren't enough (John 8:31–32).

____ Everyone's teaching should be taken at face value. If their intentions seem good, they must be alright (Matt. 7:15).

____ The most respected of righteous personas might hide a heart filled with greed and wickedness (Luke 11:39).

____ It's impossible to draw near to God in prayer and lift up songs of praise without engaging one's heart (Isa. 29:13).

____ That one moment of public recognition and honor from our peers makes every sacrifice worthwhile (Matt. 6:2).

____ The integrity of leaders doesn't really matter so long as they get the job done (Job 34:30).

____ Hypocrisy has a way of creeping in and affecting all of us if we don't guard against it (Luke 12:1).

____ Those who successfully convince others of their own
integrity find lifelong satisfaction in their achievement
(Job 20:5).

12. In the war against truth, every opportunity is taken to sow
doubt and disbelief. Lies are spun with just enough truthfulness to
make them seem reasonable. A few carefully chosen words can
throw the unprepared into confusion. What did Paul foresee happening in the church, according to Acts 20:29–31?

"ONE OF THE PRIMARY
OBJECTIVES OF EVERY
APOSTATE TEACHER IS TO
LURE PEOPLE BACK INTO THE
BONDAGE OF IMMORALITY
AFTER THEY HAVE BEEN
EXPOSED TO THE LIBERATING
TRUTH OF THE GOSPEL."

13. According to 1 Timothy 6:3–4, how does Paul dismiss those who would teach things contrary to Scripture within the church?

Apostasy speaks of abandonment, a separation, a defection—the abdication of truth altogether. They never really *believe* the truth with an undivided heart. Like tares among wheat, they have an appearance of authenticity for awhile, but they are incapable of producing any useful fruit.

An apostate is a defector from the truth—someone who has known the truth, given some show of affirmation to it, perhaps even proclaimed it for a while, but then rejected it in the end. The typical apostate may still purport to believe the truth and proclaim the truth; but in reality he opposes the truth and undermines it.

14. When false teaching goes unchallenged, it breeds more confusion and draws still more shallow and insincere people into the fold. Peter does not waste any subtlety or employ any understatements in his evaluation of the apostates of his day. How does he describe such false teachers in 2 Peter 2:18–19?

15. Jesus' teaching made the truth starkly clear, and the stark clarity of the truth was the very thing that drove them away. Why? The truth was too demanding, too unpopular, too inconvenient, too much of a threat to their own agenda, and too much of a rebuke to their sin. What does John 3:19 say drives people to reject the truth?

False teachers? Apostasy? It takes a willful naiveté to deny that such a thing could happen in our time. As a matter of fact, it is happening on a massive scale. Now is not a good time for Christians to flirt with the spirit of the age. We cannot afford to be apathetic about the truth God has put in our trust. It is our duty to guard, proclaim, and pass that truth on to the next generation.

The absolute *worst* strategy for ministering the gospel in a climate like this is for Christians to imitate the uncertainty or echo the cynicism of the postmodern perspective—and in effect drag the Bible and the gospel into it. Instead we need to affirm *against* the spirit of the age that which God has spoken with the utmost clarity, authority, and finality through His Son. And we have the infallible record of that message in Scripture.

16. What does Paul say is the root of the problem for those who are trying to establish their own righteousness, according to Romans 10:3?

17. It's tempting to live under a veneer of righteousness. It's also tempting to believe false teaching when it's so much easier to swallow than the truth. Keeping in mind what Jesus says about trying to justify ourselves before men in Luke 16:15, what choices can you make that would carry with them the esteem of God?

3

CERTAINTIES

"Many are unwilling to take a bold stand for the truth even among other Christians, in an environment where there is no serious threat against them—and the worst effect of such a stand might be that someone's feelings get hurt."

—The Truth War

*M*any self-styled evangelicals today are openly questioning whether such a thing as truth even exists. Others suppose that even if truth does exist, it can't really matter much. This type of thinking is epidemic, even among some of the evangelical movement's most popular authors and spokespersons. Some flatly refuse to stand for anything, because they have decided even Scripture isn't really clear enough to argue about.

Except for the massive scale on which such thinking has attained popularity today, and the way it is seeping into the church, such ideas themselves are really nothing new or particularly shocking. It's exactly the same attitude with which Pilate summarily dismissed Christ: "What is truth?" (John 18:38 NKJV).

1. When it comes to biblical truth—any truth—we must begin and end with God. He alone is eternal and self-existent, and He alone is the Creator of all else. He is the fountain of all truth. If you don't believe that, try defining "truth" without reference to God, and see how quickly all such definitions fail. What do the following verses say about the nature of God and truth?

Psalm 19:1–6

Psalm 19:7–11

John 14:6

Romans 2:14–15

"EVERY THOUGHT ABOUT
THE ESSENCE OF TRUTH—
WHAT IT IS, WHAT MAKES
IT TRUE, AND HOW WE
CAN POSSIBLY KNOW
ANYTHING FOR SURE,
QUICKLY MOVES US BACK
TO GOD."

Romans 11:36

Hebrews 1:1–3

2. Truth is that which is consistent with the mind, will, character, glory, and being of God. Even more to the point: truth is the self-expression of God. What does Psalm 53:1 consider to be a most foolish statement?

"CHRISTIAN MARTYRS 'FOUGHT' FOR THE TRUTH BY PROCLAIMING IT IN THE FACE OF FIERCE OPPOSITION, BY LIVING LIVES THAT GAVE TESTIMONY TO THE POWER AND GOODNESS OF TRUTH, AND BY REFUSING TO RENOUNCE OR FORSAKE THE TRUTH NO MATTER WHAT THREATS WERE MADE AGAINST THEM."

3. Truth is ontological. It is the way things really are. Reality is what it is because God declared it so and made it so. Therefore God is the author, source, determiner, governor, arbiter, ultimate standard, and final judge of all truth. What do we learn about truth in John 14:6?

4. Every true Christian should know and love the truth. In fact, a genuine love for the truth is built into saving faith. What do we learn about the relationship between truth and salvation in 2 Thessalonians 2:10?

5. A suffocating apathy about the whole concept of truth is rampant in today's society. We must foster our love for truth with diligence. What is one way in which we can do this, according to 2 Timothy 2:15?

6. What does Peter say that Scripture provides in 2 Peter 1:3?

7. According to 2 Timothy 3:15–17, what are the Scriptures able to do?

What is truth? Where does this concept come from, and why is it so basic to all human thought? Every idea we have, every relationship we cultivate, every belief we cherish, every fact we know, every argument we make, every conversation we engage in, and every thought we think presupposes that there is such a thing as "truth." The idea is an essential concept, without which the human mind could not function.

8. Postmodernism's hesitance to say anything for certain is completely antithetical to the bold confidence Scripture says is the birthright of every believer. What does Ephesians 3:12 say is ours through faith in Christ?

9. While the world resists the notion of truth, believers can take comfort in the assurance our faith gives. According to 1 Thessalonians 1:5, what gives believers this assurance?

10. Solomon's wisdom includes the exhortation to "buy the truth, and do not sell it" (Prov. 23:23 NKJV). See if you can discern which statement is true and which is false, basing your answers on the accompanying Scripture.

___ Limiting ourselves to one truth does nothing but tie us down and restrict our freedom (John 8:32).

___ Jesus always spoke the truth, but there are those who refuse to believe Him (John 8:45).

___ Truth is able to change lives (John 17:17).

___ The consequences of ignoring the truth are dire indeed (Rom. 2:8).

___ Even those who know the truth can be confused by clever lies if they're not careful (Gal. 3:1).

___ Those who stand for the truth are called the Lord's delight (Prov. 12:22).

11. While it's quite true that believing the truth entails more than the assent of the human intellect to certain propositions, it is equally true that authentic faith never involves anything less. Faith is founded on truth. What does John assure us of in 2 John 1:2?

12. What promise does the presence of the Holy Spirit carry with it, according to John 16:13?

13. It is every believer's solemn duty to resist every attack on the truth, to abhor the very thought of falsehood, and not to compromise in any way with the enemy. What does Jesus call our enemy in John 8:44?

"IN ORDER TO BE AN
EFFECTIVE WARRIOR
IN THE BATTLE
FOR TRUTH TODAY,
SEVERAL OLD-FASHIONED
CHRIST-LIKE VIRTUES
ARE ABSOLUTELY ESSENTIAL
INCLUDING BIBLICAL
DISCERNMENT, WISDOM,
FORTITUDE, DETERMINATION,
ENDURANCE, SKILL
IN HANDLING SCRIPTURE,
STRONG CONVICTIONS,
THE ABILITY TO SPEAK
CANDIDLY WITHOUT WAFFLING,
AND A WILLINGNESS
TO ENTER INTO CONFLICT."

14. History is filled with accounts of people who chose to accept torture or death rather than deny the truth. Yet today, few seem to be willing to speak up for the truth—much less die for it. What does Paul call the church in 1 Timothy 3:15?

"MULTITUDES OF 'ENLIGHTENED' EVANGELICALS HAVE WHOLEHEARTEDLY EMBRACED THE CARDINAL POSTMODERN VIRTUES— BROAD-MINDEDNESS AND DIVERSITY—WHILE DELIBERATELY SETTING ASIDE CRITICAL BIBLICAL VALUES, SUCH AS DISCERNMENT AND FIDELITY TO THE TRUTH."

The postmodern movement is marked by a distrust of logic, a distaste for certainty, and a dislike for clarity. Postmodernists don't have a very strong commitment to precisely understanding Scripture and its vital doctrines. They just want something new and fresh. They don't like the clarity and inflexibility required to deal with truth in propositional form. Propositions force us to face facts and decide whether to affirm or deny them, and that kind of clarity simply does not play well in a postmodern culture.

15. The evangelical movement has been pounded with an unrelenting barrage of outlandish ideas, philosophies, and programs. But Paul says, "You should no longer walk as the rest of the Gentiles walk, in the futility of their mind" (Eph. 4:17 NKJV). Consider what each of these verses teaches about the role of our mind in our faith.

Deuteronomy 6:5

Romans 7:25

Romans 8:6–8

Colossians 3:2

16. The battle for truth in the church has always been a very, very difficult but necessary conflict. It's a battle that engages both our hearts and minds. What does Paul say about such inner conflicts in Romans 7:23?

The church's duty has always been to confront such skepticism and answer it by clearly proclaiming the truth God has revealed in His Word. We have been given a clear message for the purpose of confronting the world's unbelief. That is what we are called, commanded, and commissioned to do (1 Cor. 12:17–31). Faithfulness to Christ demands it. We cannot sit by and simply do nothing while worldly, revisionist, and skeptical attributes about truth are infiltrating the church. We must not embrace such confusion in the name of charity, collegiality, or unity. We have to stand and fight for the truth—and be prepared to die for it—as faithful Christians always have.

17. That's not to suggest, of course, that we have *exhaustive* knowledge. But we do have infallible knowledge of what Scripture reveals, as the Spirit of God teaches us through the Word of God. What does Paul say we have been given in 1 Corinthians 2:12?

18. The fact that our knowledge grows fuller and deeper—and we all therefore change our minds about some things as we gain more and more light—doesn't mean that everything we know is uncertain, or outdated, or in need of an overhaul every few years. Why does the beloved disciple write, according to 1 John 2:20–21?

4

DOCTRINES

"The only infallible interpreter of what we see in nature or know innately in our own consciences is the explicit revelation of Scripture. Since Scripture is also the one place where we are given an infallible account of Christ, the Bible is the touchstone to which all truth-claims should be brought and by which all other truth must finally be measured."

—The Truth War

Sound doctrine? Too arcane for the average churchgoers. *Biblical exposition?* That alienates the "unchurched." *Clear preaching on sin and redemption?* Let's be careful not to subvert the self-esteem of hurting people. *The Great Commission?* Our most effective strategy has been making the church service into a massive Super Bowl party. *Serious discipleship?* Sure. There's a great series of group studies based on "I Love Lucy" episodes. Let's work our way through that. *Worship where God is recognized as high and lifted up?* Get real. We need to reach people on the level where they are.

Even at the very heart of the evangelical mainstream, where you might expect to find some commitment to biblical doctrine and at least a measure of concern about defending the faith, what you find instead is a movement utterly dominated by people whose first concern is to try to keep in step with the times in order to be relevant.

1. The same truths have always been at the heart of the Truth War—the inspiration, authority, inerrancy, and sufficiency of Scripture. What does Paul assure believers of in 2 Timothy 3:16–17?

2. All the other aspects of religious experience flow from the truth we believe and simply give expression to it. Take away the ground of truth, and all you have is fluctuating religious sentiment. What does Paul say that the truth of Scripture is able to do in 2 Timothy 3:15?

3. According to the Bible, you haven't really grasped the truth at all if there's no sense in which you know it, believe it, submit to it, and love it. See if you can discern which of the following statements is true or false, basing your answer on the accompanying Scripture.

____ Scripture can work miracles that would be otherwise impossible (Ps. 19:7).

____ For those with a taste for it, truth is sweeter than sugar and finer than gold (Ps. 19:10).

____ Truth transforms something that was dead into something everlastingly alive (John 5:24).

____ Ignoring the truth would be like bumping around in a dark room without turning on the flashlight in your hand (2 Pet. 1:19).

____ The truth we have from God is as essential for living as food is for the body (Matt. 4:4).

____ Because of truth, we've come into an inheritance beyond our wildest dreams (Acts 20:32).

____ When we heed the instructions that truth holds for us, we're promised a great reward (Ps. 19:11).

4. The Scriptures did not come into being because of the creative writing of ancient authors. God's Word is just that—His words. And in the Scriptures He reveals Himself to us. What does 2 Peter 1:21 tell us about how our Bible came to be?

5. In each of these verses, we learn something about the authorship of God's Word. Who did God use to record His Word in each?

Acts 1:16

Romans 1:2

2 Peter 3:16

6. In 1 Corinthians 10:11, why does Paul say the Scriptures were recorded?

Historically and collectively, Christians have always been in full agreement that whatever is true—whatever is objectively and ontologically true—is true whether or not any given individual understands it, likes it, or receives it as truth. In other words, because reality is created and truth is defined by God, what's really true is true for everyone, regardless of anyone's personal perspective or individual preferences.

7. As Christians, our duty is to conform all our thoughts to the truth; we are not entitled to redefine "truth" to fit our personal viewpoints, preferences, or desires. We can't ignore or discard selected truths just because we might find them hard to receive or difficult to fathom.

How should we regard the Scriptures according to 1 Thessalonians 2:13?

What prayer of the psalmist should we take as our own, as it is found in Psalm 19:14?

8. Truth is an objective reality. It exists outside of us and remains the same regardless of how we may perceive it. What does Jesus say we will find if we search the Scriptures, according to John 5:39?

Truth is never determined by looking at God's Word and asking, *What does this mean to me?* Whenever I hear someone talk like that, I'm inclined to ask, "What did the Bible mean before you existed? What does *God* mean by what He says?" Those are the proper questions to be asking. Truth and meaning are not determined by how we feel about something. The true meaning of Scripture—or anything else, for that matter—has already been determined and fixed by the mind of God. My task as interpreter is to discern that meaning.

9. Fortunately, the meaning of God's Word is neither as obscure nor as difficult to grasp as people today often pretend. Its central, essential message is plain enough for all to understand. How does Isaiah 35:8 describe the path to holiness?

10. We gain better understanding as we grow and move from a merely childlike knowledge to a more mature grasp of truth in all its richness and relationship to other truth. But truth itself does not change just because our point of view does. To what do these verses compare our appetite and apprehension for the truth?

1 Peter 2:2

1 Corinthians 3:2

Hebrews 5:12

11. The Word of God isn't just an instruction manual for life or a textbook on the Divine. What does Hebrews 4:12 remind us about the Scriptures?

12. The attempts to remodel the truth by postmodernism pose a severe danger to the heart and core of the Christian gospel. What is lost once the message is changed, according to Romans 15:4?

We must never assume that things such as a teacher's reputation, the warmth of his personality, or the majority opinion about him are perfectly safe barometers of whether his teaching is really dangerous or not. We also shouldn't imagine that common sense, intuition, or first impressions are reliable ways of determining whether this or that error poses a serious threat or not. Scripture, and Scripture alone, is the only safe guide in this area.

13. Doctrinal saboteurs inside the church have always confused more people and done more damage than open adversaries on the outside. What fact should we keep in the forefront of our minds when we listen to teaching on the Scriptures, according to 2 Peter 1:20?

"THE VISIBLE CHURCH TODAY IS FILLED WITH PEOPLE WHO HAVE DECIDED THAT BIBLICAL DISCERNMENT, DOCTRINAL BOUNDARIES, AND THE AUTHORITY OF DIVINELY REVEALED TRUTH ARE WORN-OUT RELICS OF A BYGONE ERA."

14. When the message we are brought contradicts the truth of Scripture, we should not sit idle. False teaching must be opposed and clearly refuted with the plain truth of God's Word. What does Jesus say to those in error in Matthew 22:29?

15. Paul is firm in confronting the idle talkers and deceivers. What does he say must be done in Titus 1:11?

16. Not knowing what you believe is by definition a kind of unbelief. Refusing to acknowledge and defend the revealed truth of God is a particularly stubborn and pernicious kind of unbelief. Advocating ambiguity, exalting uncertainty, or otherwise deliberately clouding the truth are also sinful ways of nurturing unbelief. What does 2 Corinthians 4:2 say we must put behind us?

The complaint of postmodernism has become a familiar refrain: "Why don't you just lighten up? Why don't you ease off the campaign to refute doctrines you disagree with? Why must you constantly critique what other Christians are teaching? After all, we all believe in the same Jesus." Scripture clearly and repeatedly warns us that not everyone who claims to believe in Jesus really does. Jesus Himself said *many* would claim to know Him who actually do not (Matt. 7:22–23).

17. These days, people are experimenting with subjective, relativistic ideas of truth—and labeling them "Christian." This signals a significant departure from biblical and historic Christianity. Carried to its necessary conclusion, it will lead inevitably to the abandonment or compromise of every essential element of the true Christian faith. What is the potent warning against tampering with the truth found in Revelation 22:18–19?

18. Have you considered just how much is at stake in the Truth War? My salvation and yours depends on a true understanding of Christ and who He is. The message of salvation is a truth, in its simplicity, which cannot—must not—be altered. What does 1 Corinthians 1:21 have to say about God's message to save us?

5

CONTENDERS

"The battlefield is the mind; the goal is the absolute triumph of truth; the priceless spoils of conquest are souls won out of the bondage of sin; the outcome is our willing submission to Christ; the highest prize is the honor given to Him as Lord; and the ultimate victory is completely His."

—The Truth War

Where are the men and women today with the courage to stand alone? The church in our age has abandoned the confrontational stance. Instead of overturning worldly wisdom with revealed truth, many Christians today are obsessed with finding areas of agreement. The goal has become *integration* rather than *confrontation*.

Those whom God uses are invariably men and women who swim against the tide. They hold strong convictions with great courage and refuse to compromise in the face of incredible opposition. David stubbornly refused to tremble before Goliath; he saw him as an affront to God. While all Israel cowered in fear, David stood alone before the enemy. Daniel, Shadrach, Meshach, and Abed-Nego all courageously refused the easy path of compromise. It surely would have cost them their lives if God had not sovereignly intervened. Yet they never wavered.

1. We live in an era when many so-called Christians have no taste for conflict and contention. Standing up for the truth as contenders for the faith requires boldness. What enabled the disciples to speak the truth with boldness according to Acts 4:31?

2. We have an urgent mandate from God Himself to do our part in the Truth War. The Holy Spirit is urging Christians to exercise caution, discernment, courage, and the will to contend earnestly for the truth. What was Paul thankful for in Philippians 1:14?

"WE WHO TRULY KNOW CHRIST AND HAVE RECEIVED THAT GIFT OF ETERNAL LIFE HAVE ALSO RECEIVED FROM HIM A CLEAR, DEFINITIVE COMMISSION TO DELIVER THE GOSPEL MESSAGE BOLDLY AS HIS AMBASSADORS."

3. Why was Isaiah encouraged not to spare anything when addressing God's people, according to Isaiah 58:1?

It is time for the faithful remnant to redraw clear lines and step up our energies in the Truth War—contending *earnestly* for the faith. In light of all the biblical commands to fight a good warfare, it is both naive and disobedient for Christians in this postmodern generation to shirk that duty.

4. We tend to think of the early church as pristine, pure, and untroubled by serious error. The truth is, it wasn't that way at all. Jude's whole point in writing the New Testament epistle that bears his name was to remind believers of their duty to fight for the truth. What is his exhortation in Jude 3?

5. Paul sounds the war cry in 2 Corinthians 10:5. What would you need to be prepared to do in order to comply with his exhortation?

6. Faithfulness to the truth is always costly in some way or another. What does Paul say is inevitable in 2 Timothy 3:12?

"THE GREEK VERB FOR *CONTEND* LITERALLY MEANS "AGONIZE AGAINST." THE WORD DESCRIBES AN INTENSIVE, ARDUOUS, DRAWN-OUT FIGHT. THERE'S NOTHING PASSIVE, PEACEFUL, OR EASY ABOUT IT."

These and similar questions are constantly heard nowadays: *Isn't it time to set aside our differences and just love one another? Rather than battling people with whom we disagree over various points of doctrine, why not stage a cordial dialogue with them, and listen to their ideas? Can't we have a friendly conversation rather than a bitter clash? Shouldn't we be congenial rather than contentious? Does the current generation really need to perpetuate the fight over beliefs and ideologies? Or can we at last declare peace and set aside all the debates over doctrine?*

7. No one who takes their place in this confrontation is going to be popular. The price of involvement is total self-sacrifice—which is just what every true Christian renders to Christ at salvation. What does Jesus ask of His followers, according to Luke 9:23–25?

8. The Bible says categorically that the Truth War is a completely different kind of war, fought with entirely different weaponry and with totally different objectives in view. What does Ephesians 6:12 say about the things we wrestle against?

9. It is every believer's solemn duty to resist every attack on the truth, to abhor the very thought of falsehood, and not to compromise in any way with the enemy, who is above all a liar and a father of lies (John 8:44). What does 2 Corinthians 10:3–4 say about our weapons and what they're capable of doing?

10. All war is ugly—it is dangerous, it is distasteful, and it is something every sane person would prefer to avoid altogether. Warfare in the spiritual realm is no different in that respect from carnal warfare; if anything, it's even more menacing. How are we equipped for this fight, according to 2 Corinthians 6:7?

This is cosmic warfare, engaging the armies of hell, which are arrayed against Christ. Their weapons consist of lies of all kinds—elaborate lies, massive philosophical lies, evil lies that appeal to humanity's fallen sinfulness, lies that inflate human pride, and lies that closely resemble the truth. Our one weapon is the simple truth of Christ as revealed in His Word.

11. Twice we find God's Truth described as the weapon it can be. What do Ephesians 6:17 and Hebrews 4:12 teach us about our armaments?

"WHEN YOU ATTACK THE LIES OF AN UTTER APOSTATE WITH THE TRUTH, YOU ARE DOING THE WORK OF GOD."

and to wield the sword of God's Word against every human speculation and every worldly hypothesis raised up against the knowledge of God. What does Paul urge believers to do in 2 Corinthians 10:5?

"PAUL DESCRIBES SPIRITUAL WARFARE AS THE DEMOLISHING OF IDEOLOGICAL FORTRESSES. HE IS DESCRIBING A BATTLE AGAINST EVIL IDEAS—THOUGHTS, ARGUMENTS, FORTRESSES MADE OF SATANIC LIES. PEOPLE ARE BASICALLY VICTIMS OF THE IDEAS, TRAPPED AND IMPRISONED BY FALSE DOCTRINES AND EVIL SYSTEMS OF THOUGHT. THE POINT OF THE WARFARE IS TO LIBERATE PEOPLE FROM THOSE FORTRESSES."

It's no mere wrangling between competing earthly ideologies. It's not simply a campaign to refine someone's religious creed or win a denominational spitting contest. It's not a battle of wits over arcane theological fine points. It's not an argument for sport. It's not like a school debate, staged to see who is more skilled or more clever in the art of argumentation. It's not merely academic in any sense. And it is certainly not a game. It is a very serious struggle to safeguard the heart and soul of truth itself, and to unleash that truth against the powers of darkness—in hopes of rescuing the eternal souls of men and women who have been unwittingly ensnared by the trap of devilish deception.

13. This is a battle we cannot wage effectively if we always try to come across to the world as merely nice, nonchalant, docile, agreeable, and fun-loving people. How does Paul say to act around those who spread serious, soul-destroying error, according to Romans 16:17?

14. We are ambassador-soldiers, reaching out to sinners with the truth even as we make every effort to destroy the lies and other forms of evil that hold them in deadly bondage. That is a perfect summary of every Christian's duty in the Truth War. What further instruction does Paul give regarding unbelievers in 2 Corinthians 6:14–15?

15. Though it may seem hard to believe, there are always people in and around the church who have heard the truth and understood it, but who have not yet embraced it and committed to it savingly. As contenders for the Truth, we must be alert. What does Paul ask us to guard against in 2 Thessalonians 3:6?

16. The church today is quite possibly *more* susceptible to false teachers, doctrinal saboteurs, and spiritual terrorism than any other generation in church history. What does Paul warn us against in 2 Timothy 3:5?

"MANY EVANGELICALS HAVE BECOME UNCOMFORTABLE WITH THE WHOLE IDEA OF MILITANCY IN DEFENSE OF THE TRUTH. THEY HAVE IN EFFECT EMBRACED THE POSTMODERN AXIOM THAT DIALOGUE IS MORALLY SUPERIOR TO DEBATE, A CONVERSATION IS INHERENTLY MORE EDIFYING THAN A CONTROVERSY, AND FELLOWSHIP IS ALWAYS BETTER THAN A FIGHT."

17. Scripture expressly warns believers not to be so blithe about the threat of spiritual terrorism. What does John ask us to be ready to do in 2 John 10–11?

Discernment demands that we hold biblical convictions with the most fervent tenacity. Titus 1:9 says a basic requirement for every elder is that he be the kind of man who "[holds] fast the faithful word as he has been taught, that he may be able, by sound doctrine, both to exhort and convict those who contradict" (NKJV). It is thus mandated by God that we take issue with error. We must refute those who contradict, or we do not fulfill our divine calling.

18. As vital as it is for us to enlist in the Truth War to do battle for our faith, it is even more important to remember why we are fighting. What did Christ expressly commend the Ephesian church for in Revelation 2:2? And what did He turn around and rebuke them for in Revelation 2:4?

6

TRUTHS

"Beloved, while I was very diligent to write to you concerning our common salvation, I found it necessary to write to you exhorting you to contend earnestly for the faith which was once for all delivered to the saint . . . . But you, beloved, remember the words which were spoken before by the apostles of our Lord Jesus Christ: how they told you that there would be mockers in the last time who would walk according to their own ungodly lusts . . . . But you, beloved, building yourselves up on your most holy faith, praying in the Holy Spirit, keep yourselves in the love of God, looking for the mercy of our Lord Jesus Christ unto eternal life."

—Jude 3, 17–18, 20–21 NKJV

It is fashionable today to characterize anyone who is concerned with biblical doctrine as pharisaical. The biblical condemnation of the Pharisees' legalism has been misread as a denunciation of doctrinal precision. And love of the truth has often been judged inherently legalistic.

But love for truth is not legalism. To caricature discernment as a sinful type of sanctimony is to sabotage the very thing the church most desperately needs today. Too many Christians are content to gaze nonchalantly at the surface of scriptural truth without plunging any deeper. They often justify their shallow indifference as a refusal to be "legalistic." Conversely, they dismiss as pharisaical narrow-mindedness any attempt to declare the truth authoritatively. Doctrine divides, therefore any concern for doctrinal matters is commonly seen as un-Christian. People concerned with discernment and sound doctrine are often accused of fostering a pharisaical, divisive attitude.

1. In verse 20 of his epistle, Jude says we must seek to remain faithful by "building yourselves up on your most holy faith" (NKJV). He is urging us to edify one another by the Word of God. To what does 1 Timothy 4:6 compare the edification of the Scriptures?

2. The phrase "your most holy faith" is a reference to sound doctrine—a right understanding of the truth as it is revealed in Scripture. Build yourself up on that, Jude says. Paul's ministry centered on getting sound doctrine into the heads and hearts of God's people. What does Colossians 1:28–29 say he strived to do?

"HERESY THAT UNDERMINES THE GOSPEL IS A FAR MORE SERIOUS SIN BECAUSE IT PLACES SOULS IN ETERNAL PERIL UNDER THE DARKNESS OF THE KIND OF LIES THAT KEEP PEOPLE IN PERMANENT BONDAGE TO THEIR SIN. THAT IS WHY THERE IS NO MORE SERIOUS ABOMINATION THAN HERESY. IT IS THE WORST AND MOST LOATHSOME KIND OF SPIRITUAL FILTH."

3. Peter says in the parallel passage: "Grow in the grace and knowledge of our Lord and Savior Jesus Christ" (2 Pet. 3:18 NKJV). We should be strengthened and become mature. This is a call to the spiritual discipline of studying the Word. What does Peter assure us God is able to do in our lives as we depend on His grace, according to 1 Peter 5:10?

Practically anyone today can advocate the most outlandish ideas or innovations and still be invited to join the evangelical conversation. But let someone seriously question whether an idea that's gaining currency in the evangelical mainstream is really biblically sound, and the person raising the concern is likely to be shouted down by others as a "heresy hunter" or dismissed as a pesky whistle-blower. That kind of backlash has occurred with such predictable regularity that the clear voices of true biblical discernment have nearly become extinct. Contemporary evangelicals have almost completely abandoned the noble practice of the Bereans, who were commended for carefully scrutinizing even the apostle Paul's teaching.

4. An almost inexhaustible gullibility has destroyed people's will to be discerning. Even the evangelical movement is shot through with confusion and error, and things are very rapidly getting worse, not better. Just what did Paul have to say about the discerning Bereans in Acts 17:11?

5. Jude urges believers to maintain their spiritual stability and equilibrium by "praying in the Holy Spirit" (Jude 20). What are we encouraged to do in Hebrews 10:22?

6. We are told to commune constantly with the Spirit of God, going before God in the power and the will of the Spirit to demonstrate our dependence on God and to cry out for His protection, His grace, His insight, and His power. How does Paul tell us to pray in Ephesians 6:18?

7. The faithful life is kept steady through means of the spiritual disciplines of study and prayer. What is the promise made to those who do so, according to Jeremiah 33:3?

8. Ultimately, only what is eternal really matters—and that means the truth matters infinitely more than any of the merely earthly things that tend to capture our attention and energies. What perspective does 1 Peter 4:7 tell us to keep in our prayers?

"PEOPLE DO NOT USUALLY BUY INTO FALSE DOCTRINE PURPOSELY. THEY ERR BECAUSE OF LAZINESS, INEPTNESS, CARELESSNESS, OR FOOLISHNESS IN HANDLING SCRIPTURE."

Clearly, spiritual ignorance and biblical illiteracy are commonplace among professing Christians. That kind of spiritual shallowness is a direct result of shallow teaching. Solid preaching with deep substance and sound doctrine is essential for Christians to grow. But churches today often teach only the barest basics—and sometimes less than that.

9. Jude further says, "keep yourselves in the love of God" (v. 21 NKJV). That is a way of reminding us to be obedient. How do the following verses make a connection between love and obedience?

John 14:21

John 15:9–10

10. Finally, Jude says, keep "looking for the mercy of our Lord Jesus Christ unto eternal life" (v. 21 NKJV). That speaks of an eager expectation of Christ's Second Coming.

What does Jesus tell us to do in Mark 13:37?

What does Paul urge us to guard against in 1 Thessalonians 5:6?

What does John exhort believers to do in Revelation 3:2?

11. Christ has graciously given us enough truth and enough understanding to equip us for every good deed—including the work of earnestly contending for the faith against deceivers who try to twist the truth of the gospel. What can we hope to be doing, then, when Jesus returns, according to Matthew 24:45–46?

12. What other reason for vigilance can be found in 1 Peter 5:8?

"BIBLE TEACHING, EVEN IN THE BEST OF VENUES TODAY, HAS BEEN DELIBERATELY DUMBED-DOWN, MADE AS BROAD AND AS SHALLOW AS POSSIBLE, OVERSIMPLIFIED, ADAPTED TO THE LOWEST COMMON DENOMINATOR—AND THEN TAILORED TO APPEAL TO PEOPLE WITH SHORT ATTENTION SPANS."

Truly biblical ministry must hold forth truths that are absolute. We must take an unmovable stance on all issues where the Bible speaks plainly. What if people don't like such dogmatism? It is necessary anyway. Sound doctrine divides, confronts, separates, judges, convicts, reproves, rebukes, exhorts, and refutes error. None of these things is very highly esteemed in postmodern thought. But the health of the church depends on our holding firmly to the truth, for where strong convictions are not tolerated, discernment cannot survive.

13. All truth sets itself against error. Where Scripture speaks, it speaks with authority. It speaks definitively. It speaks decisively. It calls for absolute conviction. See if you can discern which of the following statements is true or false, basing your answer on the accompanying Scripture.

___ Believers must resist what temptation offers and submit to God in all things (James 4:7).

___ Becoming a Christian ensures us of a life free from difficulties (Matt. 7:13–14).

___ We must be able to discern between the spirit of truth and the spirit of error (1 John 4:6).

___ It is permissible for us to keep one or two connections with the sins of our past if we're mostly good (1 Pet. 3:11).

___ Following God is a cinch. We need only do what seems like the right thing at the time (Prov. 16:25).

___ God just doesn't think about things the same way we do. His perspective is different (Isa. 55:8).

___ We are ordered to protect the truth and reject lies (Rom. 1:25).

___ We cannot claim ignorance of our sin because we know the truth (1 John 2:21).

___ Even ungodly men have good things to say. There's no harm in taking their advice (Ps. 1:1).

___ The righteous shall be blessed and the wicked will perish (Ps. 1:6).

___ Building friendships with the enemy is the best way to woo them over to our side (James 4:4).

___ There's no hurry about choosing sides in the Truth War. A little tolerance is a good thing (1 Kings 18:21).

14. It comes down to choosing. Either we believe what Scripture says and act accordingly, or we allow postmodernist thinking to lead us down the broad road to destruction. There is no middle ground. What choice was set before God's people in Joshua 24:15?

What is truth? *The Truth War* begins with that question, and my earnest hope is that the answer is clear by now: Truth is not any individual's opinion or imagination. *Truth is what God decrees.* And He has given us an infallible source of saving truth in His revealed Word.

For the true Christian, this should not be a complex issue. God's Word is what all pastors and church leaders are commanded to proclaim, in season and out of season—when it is well received and even when it is not (2 Tim. 4:2). It is what every Christian is commanded to read, study, meditate on, and divide rightly. It is what we are called and commissioned by Christ to teach and proclaim to the uttermost parts of the earth.

Leader's Guide

Chapter 1

1."This I say, therefore, and testify in the Lord, that you should no longer walk as the rest of the Gentiles walk, in the futility of their mind" (Eph. 4:17 NKJV). So often the church vainly tries to put on a bigger, flashier spectacle than the world. But that's not the war we should be fighting. We're not competing for attention. We're fighting for the truth. And to do that, we must turn our backs on the futility of worldly pursuits.

2. "For we have spent enough of our past lifetime in doing the will of the Gentiles—when we walked in lewdness, lusts, drunkenness, revelries, drinking parties, and abominable idolatries. In regard to these, they think it is strange that you do not run with them in the same flood of dissipation, speaking evil against you" (1 Pet. 4:3–4 NKJV). When we are saved, our past lifetime becomes just that—the past. We stand out from the world because of our changed behavior. Our new lives bear testimony to the changes God has wrought in our hearts. Trying to fit back into the same old lifestyle would be foolish indeed.

3. "Traitors, headstrong, haughty, lovers of pleasure rather than lovers of God" (2 Tim. 3:4 NKJV). We cannot have both. Those who love pleasure are set in direct opposition of those who love

God. We must choose. "For we ourselves were also once foolish, disobedient, deceived, serving various lusts and pleasures" (Titus 3:3 NKJV). Self-serving pleasures are put into our past once we choose to serve the Lord. "Choosing rather to suffer affliction with the people of God than to enjoy the passing pleasures of sin" (Heb. 11:25 NKJV). The pleasures that the world has to offer are definitely tempting, but we're assured that they are passing. What God offers us exceeds all else and is eternal.

4. "Do not become idolaters as were some of them. As it is written, 'The people sat down to eat and drink, and rose up to play'" (1 Cor. 10:7 NKJV). Those who are entirely caught up in the hedonistic pleasures of life have become self-serving to the point of idolatry.

5. "Their destiny is destruction, their god is their stomach, and their glory is in their shame. Their mind is on earthly things" (Phil. 3:19 NIV). One of the "beauties" of the postmodern mindset is that believers needn't deny themselves anything. Truth is bent and stretched just enough to accommodate the things we'd rather not give up. We give ourselves permission to indulge our appetites, to our shame.

6. "Now the ones that fell among thorns are those who, when they have heard, go out and are choked with cares, riches, and pleasures of life, and bring no fruit to maturity" (Luke 8:14 NKJV).

When our days are filled with the pursuit of worldly pleasures and cares, there is no room left for the good things God would have us doing instead. Our time is so choked with frivolous things that we become unfruitful in spiritual things.

7. "You are the light of the world. A city that is set on a hill cannot be hidden" (Matt. 5:14 NKJV). Camouflage is not our goal. As Christians—followers of Jesus Christ—we should stand out like a light in the darkness.

8. "Ye are a chosen generation, a royal priesthood, an holy nation, a peculiar people" (1 Pet. 2:9 KJV). Peculiar. We aren't meant to blend, to fit in, to mix well. We're to stand apart, be distinct, and bear witness to the new life grace has given us.

9. "For to this you were called, because Christ also suffered for us, leaving us an example, that you should follow His steps" (1 Pet. 2:21 NKJV). We are followers of Jesus Christ, and we should not let anything distract us from where He leads.

10. "The steps of a good man are ordered by the LORD, and He delights in his way" (Ps. 37:23 NKJV). God knows where we're going, even if we aren't quite sure. What's more, the path that lies ahead of us brings God delight. "The law of his God is in his heart; none of his steps shall slide" (Ps. 37:31 NKJV). When we cling to the truth along life's journey, we are assured of firm footing.

"Righteousness will go before Him, and shall make His footsteps our pathway" (Ps. 85:13 NKJV). We needn't worry about where to turn or what to do. The Lord's own footsteps shall serve as our path.

11. "There is therefore now no condemnation to those who are in Christ Jesus, who do not walk according to the flesh, but according to the Spirit" (Rom. 8:1 NKJV). Two ways of walking—according to the flesh, or to the Spirit. Paul urges all believers to put the flesh behind them and move forward into a new life in the Spirit.

12. T, F, T, F, T

13. "That you may walk worthy of the Lord, fully pleasing Him, being fruitful in every good work and increasing in the knowledge of God" (Col. 1:10 NKJV). Paul's hopes are a little intimidating—fully pleasing, fruitful, filled with knowledge. That's quite a lot to live up to! But it's a goal worthy of our pursuit, and one we can work toward in very practical ways. Want to please God? Study to find out what pleases Him. Want to be fruitful? Study to find out what kind of fruit God wants us to yield. And in the process of seeking these answers, you'll be growing in the knowledge of the Lord along the way. Worthy goals, indeed.

14. "We should no longer be children, tossed to and fro and carried about with every wind of doctrine, by the trickery of men, in

the cunning craftiness of deceitful plotting" (Eph. 4:14 NKJV). It's definitely not popular these days to claim to know of something for certain—to know the truth. But truth is the foundation of our heritage as Christians. Without it, our lives would never know stability. Every little thing could throw us into confusion.

15. "For the foolish person will speak foolishness, and his heart will work iniquity: to practice ungodliness, to utter error against the LORD, to keep the hungry unsatisfied, and he will cause the drink of the thirsty to fail" (Isa. 32:6 NKJV). Those who refuse to acknowledge the truth end up acting foolishly. They talk non-sense. They make sinful plans and act on them. They spout untruths. They find their chosen path leaves them dissatisfied. And they'll bring down as many with them as they can in spite of it all. We do well to guard against such people.

16. "For they being ignorant of God's righteousness, and seeking to establish their own righteousness, have not submitted to the righteousness of God" (Rom. 10:3 NKJV). All it takes to wind up in a whole mess of trouble is a little ignorance. Postmodernism lulls people into believing they can create their own truth. They try to do the right thing and live good lives, but on their own terms instead of God's.

17. "Beware lest anyone cheat you through philosophy and empty deceit, according to the tradition of men, according to the basic principles of the world, and not according to Christ" (Col. 2:8

NKJV). Paul warns that empty philosophies can cheat us. They distract us for a time, divert us from the truth, and rob us of fruitful days. We must be wise to recognize such untruths for what they are and to refuse to be taken in by them.

18. "For the time will come when they will not endure sound doctrine, but according to their own desires, because they have itching ears, they will heap up for themselves teachers; and they will turn their ears away from the truth, and be turned aside to fables" (2 Tim. 4:3–4 NKJV). People have begun to pick and choose what they will listen to and what they will believe. They will only listen to those who will tell them what they want to hear.

CHAPTER 2

1. "Nor give heed to fables and endless genealogies, which cause disputes rather than godly edification which is in faith" (1 Tim. 1:4 NKJV). Wrangling over side-issues and non-issues only serves to distract from the things that will truly edify believers. "O Timothy! Guard what was committed to your trust, avoiding the profane and idle babblings and contradictions of what is falsely called knowledge" (1 Tim. 6:20 NKJV). Philosophical babble can run in useless circles and even chip away at one's grasp on the truth. Paul warned Timothy to guard against the lure of worldly knowledge.

2. F, T, F, F, T, F, T, T, F, T

3. "Do not be carried about with various and strange doctrines. For it is good that the heart be established by grace" (Heb. 13:9 NKJV). Our hearts cannot be distracted and carried away by false teachings if they have been first established in the truth. The writer of Hebrews says that it's a good thing to have one's heart established by grace.

4. "If the world hates you, you know that it hated Me before it hated you. If you were of the world, the world would love its own. Yet because you are not of the world, but I chose you out of the world, therefore the world hates you" (John 15:18–19 NKJV). We

don't need to change in order to attract the attention or admiration of unbelievers. We don't have to do things their way to win the respect of unbelievers. The gospel doesn't have to be tweaked or updated to give it greater appeal. Why not? Because it won't work. The same world that hates Jesus will hate us. That will never change.

5. "Now I urge you, brethren, note those who cause divisions and offenses, contrary to the doctrine which you learned, and avoid them. For those who are such do not serve our Lord Jesus Christ, but their own belly, and by smooth words and flattering speech deceive the hearts of the simple" (Rom. 16:17–18 NKJV). False teachers serve themselves. They convince people to believe them by their persuasive skills—"smooth words and flattering speech." Those who are most vulnerable are the simple, who are perhaps too trusting and definitely too ignorant of the truth. And Paul says to make a note of those who are working falsely and to avoid them.

6. "So they come to you as people do, they sit before you as My people, and they hear your words, but they do not do them; for with their mouth they show much love, but their hearts pursue their own gain. Indeed you are to them as a very lovely song of one who has a pleasant voice and can play well on an instrument; for they hear your words, but they do not do them" (Ezek. 33:31–32 NKJV). The hypocrites fit right in. They join with God's people. They sit and they listen. They say they love God. But their hearts and their lives remain unchanged. They like listening to the truth, but when it comes down to it, they will not do as they are told. They nod and smile, but refuse to change.

7. "Hypocrites! Well did Isaiah prophesy about you, saying: 'These people draw near to Me with their mouth, and honor Me with their lips, but their heart is far from Me. And in vain they worship Me, teaching as doctrines the commandments of men'" (Matt. 15:7–9 NKJV). If you listen to what these people say, you'd think they had vibrant spiritual lives, but their words are proven empty. Nice words cannot fool the One who can see the truth in one's heart.

8. "But be doers of the word, and not hearers only, deceiving yourselves" (James 1:22 NKJV). It isn't enough to know about the truth. It's not enough to listen to it, think about it, study it, or even sing about it. James says that the truth doesn't do any good in our lives if we don't live by it. We need to be doers of the word.

9. "Having a form of godliness but denying its power. And from such people turn away!" (2 Tim. 3:5 NKJV). Those who are keeping up the appearance of righteousness have a "form of godliness," but the truth of their hypocrisy becomes evident. We are to note such people and turn away from them.

10. "The way of a fool is right in his own eyes, but he who heeds counsel is wise" (Prov. 12:15 NKJV). The foolish person uses his or her own understanding as a basis for living. He or she does whatever seems right at the time. "He has said in his heart, 'God has forgotten; He hides His face; He will never see'" (Ps. 10:11 NKJV). Such people rationalize their behavior by telling themselves that God isn't paying attention, doesn't see, or just doesn't care. "Who, knowing the righteous judgment of God, that those who

practice such things are deserving of death, not only do the same but also approve of those who practice them" (Rom. 1:32 NKJV). Willful disobedience. Even though they know they are sinning, they not only choose to continue, but urge others to join in.

11. T, T, F, T, T, F, F, F, T, F

12. "For I know this, that after my departure savage wolves will come in among you, not sparing the flock" (Acts 20:29 NKJV). Those who deceive with their falsehoods, contradictions, distortions, and misrepresentations are called wolves by Paul—wolves in sheep's clothing (Matt. 7:15).

13. "If anyone teaches otherwise and does not consent to wholesome words, even the words of our Lord Jesus Christ, and to the doctrine which accords with godliness, he is proud, knowing nothing, but is obsessed with disputes and arguments over words" (1 Tim. 6:3–4 NKJV). Paul dismisses those who speak contrary to Jesus' words as prideful people who don't know what they're talking about. Instead, they take pleasure in stirring up debates.

14. "For when they speak great swelling words of emptiness, they allure through the lusts of the flesh, through lewdness, the ones who have actually escaped from those who live in error. While they promise them liberty, they themselves are slaves of corruption; for by whom a person is overcome, by him also he is brought into bondage" (2 Pet. 2:18–19 NKJV). This verse is packed with powerful, descriptive words. Peter talks about empty words that allure. He tells us that the glowing promises of freedom will only end in

corruption and slavery. False teachers lead those who follow them into bondage.

15. "And this is the condemnation, that the light has come into the world, and men loved darkness rather than light, because their deeds were evil" (John 3:19 NKJV). It's uncomfortable to face up to your own sin, and the light of the truth doesn't spare any punches. Suddenly, people were faced with a truth they didn't want to hear. So they rejected it.

16. "For they being ignorant of God's righteousness, and seeking to establish their own righteousness, have not submitted to the righteousness of God" (Rom. 10:3 NKJV). They refuse to submit to God's righteousness, so the root of the problem is rebellion.

17. "You are those who justify yourselves before men, but God knows your hearts. For what is highly esteemed among men is an abomination in the sight of God" (Luke 16:15 NKJV). Jesus tells us that the things that bring high esteem from men are often the very things that are abominations in God's sight. That forces us to make a choice. We cannot please both God and men. Answers here will vary depending on circumstances, but we need to make choices that will be praiseworthy in God's eyes, not the world's.

CHAPTER 3

1. Psalm 19:1–6 ~ Every truth revealed in nature was authored by Him. Psalm 19:7–11 ~ God gave us the perfect, infallible truth of Scripture. John 14:6 ~ God sent Jesus, the embodiment of truth. Romans 2:14–15 ~ We've been given consciences to perceive truth. Romans 11:36 ~ God is the source of all that exists. Hebrews 1:1–3 ~ Jesus is the culmination of divine revelation.

2. "The fool has said in his heart, 'There is no God'" (Ps. 53:1 NKJV). Once someone denies God, logical consistency will ultimately force that person to deny all truth.

3. "I am the way, the truth, and the life" (John 14:6 NKJV). Not only is God the author, source, and determiner of truth, He *is* truth. It is so essential to His nature, it is one of His names.

4. "And with all unrighteous deception among those who perish, because they did not receive the love of the truth, that they might be saved" (2 Thess. 2:10 NKJV). We are saved when we "receive the love of the truth." We could not receive the gift of salvation if we did not first know, understand, accept, and cling to the truth that it rests upon.

5. "Be diligent to present yourself approved to God, a worker who does not need to be ashamed, rightly dividing the word of truth" (2 Tim. 2:15 NKJV). Diligent study of the Scriptures will certainly foster our love for the truth. Paul urges students of the Word to be diligent in learning to "rightly divide" its message.

6. "As His divine power has given to us all things that pertain to life and godliness, through the knowledge of Him who called us by glory and virtue" (2 Pet. 1:3 NKJV). Peter says that the Word of truth provides all things that pertain to godly life and living.

7. "From childhood you have known the Holy Scriptures, which are able to make you wise for salvation through faith which is in Christ Jesus. All Scripture is given by inspiration of God, and is profitable for doctrine, for reproof, for correction, for instruction in righteousness, that the man of God may be complete, thoroughly equipped for every good work" (2 Tim. 3:15–17 NKJV). Paul points to Timothy's own experience, as the Scriptures were able to bring him to salvation through faith. He then tells us that the inspired Word is profitable for doctrine, reproof, correction, instruction, and equipping.

8. "In whom we have boldness and access with confidence through faith in Him" (Eph. 3:12 NKJV). We have access to God. We have confidence in Him. And we have boldness to approach Him. We live with security, assurance, peace, and understanding.

9. "For our gospel did not come to you in word only, but also in power, and in the Holy Spirit and in much assurance" (1 Thess. 1:5 NKJV). We have the Word. We have the Spirit. And we have power. Such assurance is wrought by the Spirit of God Himself in those who believe.

10. F, T, T, T, T, T

11. "Because of the truth which abides in us and will be with us forever" (2 John 1:2 NKJV). Truth abides in us eternally.

12. "When He, the Spirit of truth, has come, He will guide you into all truth; for He will not speak on His own authority, but whatever He hears He will speak; and He will tell you things to come" (John 16:13 NKJV). Not only is the Holy Spirit the Spirit of truth, but He comes to teach us. He guides us toward the truth—an unerring guide for our hearts.

13. "He was a murderer from the beginning, and does not stand in the truth, because there is no truth in him. When he speaks a lie, he speaks from his own resources, for he is a liar and the father of it" (John 8:44 NKJV). Deception is Satan's mark and trade. He is the Father of Lies.

14. "I write so that you may know how you ought to conduct yourself in the house of God, which is the church of the living God, the pillar and ground of the truth" (1 Tim. 3:15 NKJV). The church is the pillar of truth!

15. "You shall love the LORD your God with all your heart, with all your soul, and with all your strength" (Deut. 6:5 NKJV). We can love God with our minds. "So then, with the mind I myself serve the law of God, but with the flesh the law of sin" (Rom. 7:25 NKJV). We can serve the law with our minds—obedience. "For to be carnally minded is death, but to be spiritually minded is life and peace. Because the carnal mind is enmity against God; for it is not subject to the law of God, nor indeed can be. So then, those who are in the flesh cannot please God" (Rom. 8:6–8 NKJV). We can choose to please God with our minds. "Set your mind on things above, not on things on the earth" (Col. 3:2 NKJV). We can give our thoughts, our meditations, and our attention to godly things.

16. "But I see another law in my members, warring against the law of my mind, and bringing me into captivity to the law of sin which is in my members" (Rom. 7:23 NKJV). Our minds are a battlefield. Postmodernist ideas and ideals have seeped in and muddied the truth. When confronted with confusing doctrines, it becomes harder and harder to give a thoughtful, biblical response.

17. "Now we have received, not the spirit of the world, but the Spirit who is from God, that we might know the things that have

been freely given to us by God" (1 Cor. 2:12 NKJV). We may not know everything, but we know enough. Scripture provides everything we need for life and godliness.

18. "But you have an anointing from the Holy One, and you know all things. I have not written to you because you do not know the truth, but because you know it, and that no lie is of the truth" (1 John 2:20–21 NKJV). John writes to remind us of what we know to be true. He affirms the truth—confirms it, and by doing so encourages us to conform to it.

CHAPTER 4

1. "All Scripture is given by inspiration of God, and is profitable for doctrine, for reproof, for correction, for instruction in righteousness, that the man of God may be complete, thoroughly equipped for every good work" (2 Tim. 3:16–17 NKJV). The Bible isn't just a piece of history or literature. It is truth. Paul reminds believers that Scripture is inspired by God Himself, and when we take it in we are made complete.

2. "From childhood you have known the Holy Scriptures, which are able to make you wise for salvation through faith which is in Christ Jesus" (2 Tim. 3:15 NKJV). Scripture is our starting point. It is where truth can be found. Paul points to the Holy Scriptures and reminds Timothy this is where it all began. Only the truth can make us wise enough to find the faith for salvation.

3. Each of these statements is true.

4. "For prophecy never came by the will of man, but holy men of God spoke as they were moved by the Holy Spirit" (2 Pet. 1:21 NKJV). It was not man, but God Himself who determined what should be written. The Spirit moved the writers of His words, inspiring the very words they would record.

5. "Men and brethren, this Scripture had to be fulfilled, which the Holy Spirit spoke before by the mouth of David" (Acts 1:16 NKJV). All of David's writings, including his many psalms, are Spirit-inspired. "Which He promised before through His prophets in the Holy Scriptures" (Rom. 1:2 NKJV). The prophets of the Old Testament era were each inspired by God in what they wrote. "As also in all his epistles, speaking in them of these things, in which are some things hard to understand, which untaught and unstable people twist to their own destruction, as they do also the rest of the Scriptures" (2 Pet. 3:16 NKJV). Here we find Peter equating Paul's epistles with the rest of the Scriptures. Even Peter recognized Paul's writing as inspired.

6. "Now all these things happened to them as examples, and they were written for our admonition, upon whom the ends of the ages have come" (1 Cor. 10:11 NKJV). The Bibles we hold today are filled with examples for living and admonitions from the Lord Himself on how to live in a way pleasing to Him.

7. "For this reason we also thank God without ceasing, because when you received the word of God which you heard from us, you welcomed it not as the word of men, but as it is in truth, the word of God, which also effectively works in you who believe" (1 Thess. 2:13 NKJV). The Bible isn't something we can approach with a "take it or leave it" mindset or even a "take it with a grain of salt" attitude. We must take it as what it is—God's truth. "Let the words of my mouth and the meditation of my heart be acceptable in Your sight, O LORD, my strength and my Redeemer" (Ps. 19:14 NKJV). As we seek to conform our lives to the truth we

find, we should echo David's prayer—may I be acceptable in Your sight, O Lord.

8. "You search the Scriptures, for in them you think you have eternal life; and these are they which testify of Me" (John 5:39 NKJV). The Pharisees had been searching the Scriptures continually, yet they missed the truth that could be found there. Why? Their perceptions were wrong. Jesus assures us that when we study the Word, we will find Him there.

9. "A highway shall be there, and a road, and it shall be called the Highway of Holiness. The unclean shall not pass over it, but it shall be for others. Whoever walks the road, although a fool, shall not go astray" (Isa. 35:8 NKJV). There is no chance of even the simplest of souls, once they find the path, wandering off it again. The message of salvation is clear enough even for a child to understand.

10. "As newborn babes, desire the pure milk of the word, that you may grow thereby" (1 Pet. 2:2 NKJV). Here we find the Word described as the milk necessary for growth. "I fed you with milk and not with solid food; for until now you were not able to receive it, and even now you are still not able" (1 Cor. 3:2 NKJV). Here we find the idea of growing up to need more than simple things as we are able to grasp more difficult aspects of the truth. "For though by this time you ought to be teachers, you need someone to teach you again the first principles of the oracles of God; and you have come to need milk and not solid food" (Heb. 5:12 NKJV). A steady

diet is necessary to keep growing, and when we neglect the truth we need to be reminded of the first things all over again.

11. "For the word of God is living and powerful, and sharper than any two-edged sword, piercing even to the division of soul and spirit, and of joints and marrow, and is a discerner of the thoughts and intents of the heart" (Heb. 4:12 NKJV). The Word of God itself is living. We should never underestimate its power to touch us, pierce us, or change us.

12. "For whatever things were written before were written for our learning, that we through the patience and comfort of the Scriptures might have hope" (Rom. 15:4 NKJV). The things we were meant to learn are lost to us if the message of the Scriptures is changed or ignored. Paul reminds us that the Word of God brings us comfort and hope. These are too precious to lose for the sake of "updating" faith for the masses.

13. "Knowing this first, that no prophecy of Scripture is of any private interpretation" (2 Pet. 1:20 NKJV). God's truth speaks for itself. Those who would twist the Scriptures to change their meaning are not to be trusted.

14. "Jesus answered and said to them, 'You are mistaken, not knowing the Scriptures nor the power of God'" (Matt. 22:29

NKJV). Be prepared to confront false doctrine with the truth. Of course, being able to recognize mistakes requires us to know the truth in the first place. Jesus' words can also serve as an encouragement to know the Scriptures ourselves.

15. "Whose mouths must be stopped" (Titus 1:11 NKJV). Paul's statement about stopping the mouths of false teachers has both a tone of authority and a settled certainty which may sound less-than-politically-correct to postmodern ears. This is not a message well suited for our age, but that doesn't make it any less true. Scripture has always been contrary to worldly culture.

16. "But we have renounced the hidden things of shame, not walking in craftiness nor handling the word of God deceitfully, but by manifestation of the truth commending ourselves to every man's conscience in the sight of God" (2 Cor. 4:2 NKJV). In a time when ambiguity, uncertainty, and a clouding of the truth are normal, we are exhorted to walk with a clean conscience before God. Paul says to handle the word of God without deceit, craftiness, or shamefulness.

17. "For I testify to everyone who hears the words of the prophecy of this book: If anyone adds to these things, God will add to him the plagues that are written in this book; and if anyone takes away from the words of the book of this prophecy, God shall take away his part from the Book of Life, from the holy city, and from the things which are written in this book" (Rev. 22:18–19 NKJV). These words carry with them the weight of truth. This is no empty threat.

Scripture is not to be added to—slipping in a few rules to suit our own agendas. Nor is it to be taken from—glossing over the exhortations that inconvenience us or make us uncomfortable. God's Word is truth and as such it stands unchanged.

18. "For since, in the wisdom of God, the world through wisdom did not know God, it pleased God through the foolishness of the message preached to save those who believe" (1 Cor. 1:21 NKJV). The truth of the message may seem like foolishness to some, but that doesn't change the immutable fact that it is the truth. We have the truth—this message that has been preached—so that we who believe can be saved. Those who stand up for the truth and defend it make it possible for more to hear that message and be saved.

CHAPTER 5

1. "When they had prayed, the place where they were assembled together was shaken; and they were all filled with the Holy Spirit, and they spoke the word of God with boldness" (Acts 4:31 NKJV). If we are to contend for the sake of the truth, we need boldness. The disciples found boldness when they had been filled with the Spirit. God supplies our needs, even the need for boldness.

2. "And most of the brethren in the Lord, having become confident by my chains, are much more bold to speak the word without fear" (Phil. 1:14 NKJV). If we are to move into this war with courage and confidence, we need God-supplied boldness. Paul was thankful that Christians were able to speak about the Lord without fear. He was thankful for their boldness.

3. "Cry aloud, spare not; lift up your voice like a trumpet; tell My people their transgression, and the house of Jacob their sins" (Isa. 58:1 NKJV). Scripture never pulls any punches when it comes to confronting error. In this verse, God has commanded Isaiah to speak the truth to His people—loud and clear, sparing no one's feelings, and without apology.

4. "Beloved, while I was very diligent to write to you concerning our common salvation, I found it necessary to write to you exhorting you to contend earnestly for the faith which was once

for all delivered to the saints" (Jude 3 NKJV). The whole book of Jude could be called a war cry. Jesus' brother finds himself compelled to stir up believers to contend earnestly for the faith.

5. "Casting down arguments and every high thing that exalts itself against the knowledge of God, bringing every thought into captivity to the obedience of Christ" (2 Cor. 10:5 NKJV). In order to do as Paul asks, we must first be able to recognize false doctrines and worldly mindsets. Then, we must be willing to confront them for what they are, showing them to be contrary to Scripture. In order to do that, we must have enough grasp of the truth to communicate it clearly. Simply put, we need discernment, boldness, and knowledge.

6. "Yes, and all who desire to live godly in Christ Jesus will suffer persecution" (2 Tim. 3:12 NKJV). Stepping up to become a contender for the faith will never win you any popularity contests. It's a war for the truth, and we are *commanded* to participate in that battle. It is not a duty any faithful Christian can shirk.

7. "If anyone desires to come after Me, let him deny himself, and take up his cross daily, and follow Me. For whoever desires to save his life will lose it, but whoever loses his life for My sake will save it. For what profit is it to a man if he gains the whole world, and is himself destroyed or lost?" (Luke 9:23–25 NKJV). We're promised that such a sacrifice will always be worthwhile, and our final triumph is likewise guaranteed—because we are "preserved in Jesus Christ."

8. "For we do not wrestle against flesh and blood, but against principalities, against powers, against the rulers of the darkness of this age, against spiritual hosts of wickedness in the heavenly places" (Eph. 6:12 NKJV). It is spiritual warfare, and we are on one side or the other. There is no middle ground—no safe zone for the uncommitted.

9. "For though we walk in the flesh, we do not war according to the flesh. For the weapons of our warfare are not carnal but mighty in God for pulling down strongholds" (2 Cor. 10:3–4 NKJV). In this war, earthly weapons are useless. Paul says that the weapons we are able to yield in this battle for the Truth are mighty enough to pull down Satan's strongholds.

10. "By the word of truth, by the power of God, by the armor of righteousness on the right hand and on the left" (2 Cor. 6:7 NKJV). In this dangerous confrontation, we can stand with confidence because of the way we are equipped. We stand boldly, armed with the word of truth, the power of God, and the armor of righteousness.

11. "The sword of the Spirit, which is the word of God" (Eph. 6:17 NKJV). "For the word of God is living and powerful, and sharper than any two-edged sword" (Heb. 4:12 NKJV). God's word is an offensive weapon—sharp and quick—and our best defense— unbreakable and untiring.

12. "Casting down arguments and every high thing that exalts itself against the knowledge of God, bringing every thought into captivity to the obedience of Christ" (2 Cor. 10:5 NKJV). If we mean to contend for the faith, we must be prepared. Paul encourages us to ready ourselves in this way.

13. "Now I urge you, brethren, note those who cause divisions and offenses, contrary to the doctrine which you learned, and avoid them" (Rom. 16:17 NKJV). We are not to build relationships with false teachers. Paul advocates giving them a wide berth.

14. "Do not be unequally yoked together with unbelievers. For what fellowship has righteousness with lawlessness? And what communion has light with darkness? And what accord has Christ with Belial? Or what part has a believer with an unbeliever?" (2 Cor. 6:14–15 NKJV). No matter how much we reach out to those who do not believe, there is a line that is drawn. Not only do we avoid false teachers, we are not to "yoke" ourselves with nonbelievers. Close friendships cannot be built between the light and the darkness.

15. "But we command you, brethren, in the name of our Lord Jesus Christ, that you withdraw from every brother who walks disorderly and not according to the tradition which he received from us" (2 Thess. 3:6 NKJV). Christians are not supposed to be gullible. We are not to turn a blind eye to the danger. We are not to have fellowship with the unfruitful works of darkness,

but rather expose them (Eph. 5:11). We simply cannot be all-embracing without allowing false teachers to infiltrate and be destructive. And that danger is both real and imminent.

16. "Having a form of godliness but denying its power. And from such people turn away!" (2 Tim. 3:5 NKJV). When something *looks* righteous and *sounds* righteous, we must have biblical discernment to know if it is truly righteous or if it merely has a "form of godliness." Biblical ignorance within the church may well be deeper and more widespread than at any other time since the Protestant Reformation.

17. "If anyone comes to you and does not bring this doctrine, do not receive him into your house nor greet him; for he who greets him shares in his evil deeds" (2 John 10–11 NKJV). Warfare is always serious, but this is the battle of the ages for the highest of prizes, and therefore it requires of us the utmost diligence. Mature wisdom and careful discernment become absolutely crucial for every Christian. Deadly error is often mixed with some truth. Therein lies the seduction.

18. "I know your works, your labor, your patience, and that you cannot bear those who are evil. And you have tested those who say they are apostles and are not, and have found them liars" (Rev. 2:2 NKJV). Jesus commended the Ephesians for examining the claims of certain false apostles and exposing them as liars. But Christ also rebuked the doctrinally sound Ephesians for departing from their

first love (2:4). We're not merely in the fight for the thrill of vanquishing some foe or winning some argument, but out of a genuine love for Christ, who is the living, breathing embodiment of all that we hold true and worth fighting for.

CHAPTER 6

1. "If you instruct the brethren in these things, you will be a good minister of Jesus Christ, nourished in the words of faith and of the good doctrine which you have carefully followed" (1 Tim. 4:6 NKJV). Scripture is nourishment for the soul.

2. "Him we preach, warning every man and teaching every man in all wisdom, that we may present every man perfect in Christ Jesus. To this end I also labor, striving according to His working which works in me mightily" (Col. 1:28–29 NKJV). Paul preached and taught and warned—laboring with love and determination.

3. "May the God of all grace, who called us to His eternal glory by Christ Jesus, after you have suffered a while, perfect, establish, strengthen, and settle you" (1 Pet. 5:10 NKJV). We need to be built up and edified, and this is a work that God is able to do in our hearts. Peter says that He who called us is able to perfect, establish, strengthen, and settle us.

4. "These were more fair-minded than those in Thessalonica, in that they received the word with all readiness, and searched the Scriptures daily to find out whether these things were so" (Acts 17:11 NKJV). Paul praises the Bereans as fair-minded. Their clear thinking, eagerness, and attention to details left quite an impression on the apostle.

5. "Let us draw near with a true heart in full assurance of faith, having our hearts sprinkled from an evil conscience and our bodies washed with pure water" (Heb. 10:22 NKJV). Draw near to God in prayer.

6. "Praying always with all prayer and supplication in the Spirit, being watchful to this end with all perseverance and supplication for all the saints" (Eph. 6:18 NKJV). Pray with perseverance, pray constantly, and watch while you pray.

7. "Call to Me, and I will answer you, and show you great and mighty things, which you do not know" (Jer. 33:3 NKJV). We are promised that when we pray, God will hear and answer. What's more, the answers He brings will be great—surprising things we may not have ever considered possible: "Him who is able to do exceedingly abundantly above all that we ask or think" (Eph. 3:20 NKJV).

8. "But the end of all things is at hand; therefore be serious and watchful in your prayers" (1 Pet. 4:7 NKJV). All these earthly things that distract and beguile us are fleeting. Only eternal things really matter. So Peter calls us to be serious in our prayer lives—serious and watchful because the end is near.

9. "He who has My commandments and keeps them, it is he who loves Me. And he who loves Me will be loved by My Father, and

I will love him and manifest Myself to him" (John 14:21 NKJV). "As the Father loved Me, I also have loved you; abide in My love. If you keep My commandments, you will abide in My love, just as I have kept My Father's commandments and abide in His love" (John 15:9–10 NKJV). Love and obedience go hand in hand. If you truly love Christ, of course you will do as He asks.

10. "And what I say to you, I say to all: Watch!" (Mark 13:37 NKJV). Jesus says to watch. "Therefore let us not sleep, as others do, but let us watch and be sober" (1 Thess. 5:6 NKJV). Paul says not to grow weary as we watch, nor allow ourselves to be distracted from our purpose. "Be watchful, and strengthen the things which remain, that are ready to die, for I have not found your works perfect before God" (Rev. 3:2 NKJV). As we watch, we must take time to strengthen those things that have eternal value.

11. "Who then is a faithful and wise servant, whom his master made ruler over his household, to give them food in due season? Blessed is that servant whom his master, when he comes, will find so doing" (Matt. 24:45–46 NKJV). In the war for the Truth, as with all aspects of life, we should want to be found doing God's work faithfully when He returns for us.

12. "Be sober, be vigilant; because your adversary the devil walks about like a roaring lion, seeking whom he may devour" (1 Pet. 5:8 NKJV). We watch with expectation, but we also watch because there is danger close at hand. Our earnest dedication to

sound doctrine and prayer help us to stave off the advances of the enemy.

13. T, F, T, F, F, T, T, T, F, T, F, F

14. "Choose for yourselves this day whom you will serve, whether the gods which your fathers served that were on the other side of the River, or the gods of the Amorites, in whose land you dwell. But as for me and my house, we will serve the LORD" (Josh. 24:15 NKJV). Choose whom you will serve. Will you serve yourself, or will you choose to serve the Lord?

The MacArthur Bible Study Series

Revised and updated, the MacArthur Study Guide Series continues to be one of the bestselling study guide series on the market today. For small group or individual use, intriguing questions and new material take the participant deeper into God's Word.

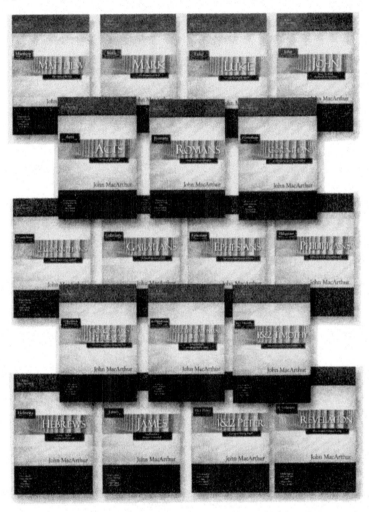

Available at your local Christian Bookstore or www.thomasnelson.com